W9-BNF-560

Looking at . . .
Ankylosaurus
A Dinosaur from the CRETACEOUS Period

Weekly Reader® BOOKS

Published by arrangement with Gareth Stevens, Inc.
Newfield Publications is a federally registered trademark
of Newfield Publications, Inc. Weekly Reader is a federally
registered trademark of Weekly Reader Corporation.

Library of Congress Cataloging-in-Publication Data

Brown, Mike, 1947-
    Looking at -- Ankylosaurus/written by Mike Brown; illustrated by Tony Gibbons.
       p. cm. -- (The New dinosaur collection)
    Includes index.
    ISBN 0-8368-1083-X
    1. Ankylosaurus—Juvenile literature. [1. Ankylosaurus. 2. Dinosaurs.] I. Gibbons,
Tony, ill. II. Title. III. Series.
QE862.O65B76   1994
567.9'7--dc20   93-37055

This North American edition first published in 1994 by
Gareth Stevens Publishing
1555 North RiverCenter Drive, Suite 201
Milwaukee, Wisconsin 53212 USA

This U.S. edition © 1994 by Gareth Stevens, Inc. Created with original
© 1993 by Quartz Editorial Services, Premier House, 112 Station Road,
Edgware HA8 7AQ U.K.

Consultant: Dr. David Norman, Director of the Sedgwick Museum of Geology,
University of Cambridge, England.

Additional artwork by Clare Heronneau.

All rights reserved. No part of this book may be reproduced, stored in a
retrieval system, or transmitted in any form or by any means, electronic,
mechanical, photocopying, or otherwise, without the prior written
permission of the copyright holder.

Printed in the United States of America

Weekly Reader Books Presents

Looking at . . . Ankylosaurus

A Dinosaur from the CRETACEOUS Period

by Mike Brown
Illustrated by Tony Gibbons

THE NEW
DINOSAUR
COLLECTION

Gareth Stevens Publishing
MILWAUKEE

Contents

5   Introducing **Ankylosaurus**

6   Armored tank

8   Tough skeleton

10   Powerful weapons

12   **Ankylosaurus** discovered

14   The last dinosaurs

16   Desert storm

18   Self-defense

20   **Ankylosaurus** and cousins

22   **Ankylosaurus** data

24   Glossary and Index

Introducing Ankylosaurus

Take a trip back in time to many millions of years ago. Imagine a large clump of high bushes. All is quiet until you hear the noise of something tugging at the leaves. As you move the branches aside, you come face-to-face with a big, heavy creature covered with all kinds of bony scales and spines.

It is an **Ankylosaurus** (AN-KY-LO-SAW-RUS), one of the most unusual dinosaurs of all time. It lived toward the end of the Cretaceous Period, about 70 million years ago.

Ankylosaurus was a very peaceful animal that ate only plants. This does not mean, however, that it could not defend itself against its enemies when it had to.

What did **Ankylosaurus** do when it was attacked by an enemy? What was the purpose of the large bony club at the end of its tail?

And how big was this creature? Read on to find out what kind of dinosaur **Ankylosaurus** was and how it survived in its dangerous world.

Armored tank

Many scientists have compared **Ankylosaurus** with an army tank. You can see how strongly built a tank is in the picture. It has very thick steel walls to protect the soldiers inside from bullets and explosions. Like a tank, **Ankylosaurus** was also powerfully built. To protect its head, neck, back, and sides, the dinosaur grew its own tough body armor.

But **Ankylosaurus**'s armor was not smooth like the sides of a tank. Instead, it was made up of many small, bony pieces, or nodules, set into the skin. Each nodule had a raised, knobby point in the center to give extra protection to this dinosaur. The nodules were covered with horny scales and were fused, or joined, together in bands.

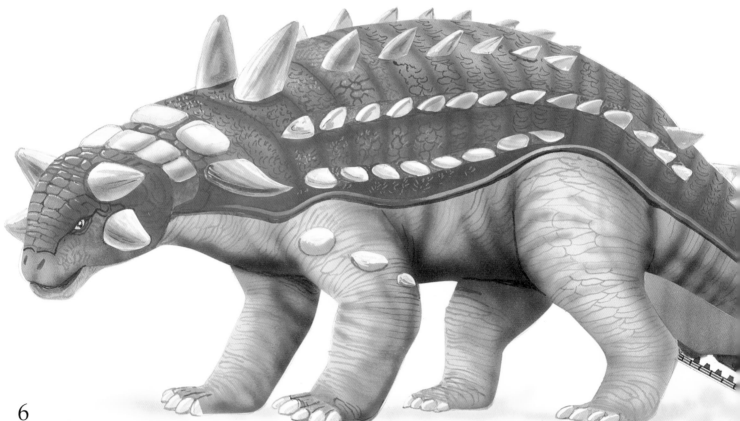

This is why the creature was called **Ankylosaurus**, a name that means "fused reptile."

All this armor was very heavy. **Ankylosaurus** weighed over two tons — almost half as much as an African elephant. It was long, as well, measuring up to 35 feet (10.7 meters) — more than the length of a bus.

Ankylosaurus also had hard, sharp spines sticking out from its back. Long, sharp spines ran around its sides, too.

The only spot on **Ankylosaurus**'s body that was not protected by its body armor was the soft belly underneath.

Enemies could sometimes take advantage of this by pushing the dinosaur onto its back and then attacking this soft area.

But, most of the time, the thought of trying to find a way through **Ankylosaurus**'s armor-plated body would have been too much for predators. Even the most vicious meat-eating dinosaurs, such as **Tyrannosaurus rex** (TIE-RAN-OH-SAW-RUS RECKS), might have thought twice before daring to attack **Ankylosaurus**.

They would have preferred to look elsewhere for their victims, choosing smaller dinosaurs that could not protect themselves as well.

Tough skeleton

The skeleton of **Ankylosaurus** reveals that it was a large and tough animal.

The most unusual part of this dinosaur's skeleton was the mighty club at the end of the tail. This club was as large as **Ankylosaurus**'s head. It was made of chunks of bone that were fused together.

Ankylosaurus had a wide, toothless beak for ripping leaves off branches. The teeth in its mouth were small and weak. **Ankylosaurus** used them for chewing plants and soft vegetation. It had a bony shelf between its nose and mouth.

This club made a powerful weapon for **Ankylosaurus** to swing at its enemies.

This shelf allowed the dinosaur to chew food and breathe at the same time. Human beings can do this, but modern reptiles cannot.

The skull was broad and covered by chunks of bone. The jaws, too, were protected by slabs of bone. **Ankylosaurus**'s head was well defended against predators; it even had bony eyelids! These protected its delicate eyes against the sharp claws of an attacker.

Ankylosaurus had strong legs. You can tell this by looking at the thick bones. Its legs had to support the heavy armor plating as well as **Ankylosaurus**'s heavy body.

But **Ankylosaurus** was not a slow, lumbering creature. It could move surprisingly fast by taking long strides on its strong legs.

Ankylosaurus's feet were very sturdy. It had five toes on its front feet and four toes on its back feet. If it found itself in danger and was unable to run away, **Ankylosaurus** could have bent its legs and dug its claws into the ground. In this way, its soft belly would have been protected, and an attacker would have been presented with **Ankylosaurus**'s tough, bony upper body.

The numerous bony plates and spines on **Ankylosaurus**'s back and tail were not truly part of its skeleton. They were embedded in its skin and were not attached to the animal's spine or ribs.

Powerful weapons

Plant-eating dinosaurs had plenty of enemies among the terrifying carnivores. Because of this, they had to develop means of defending themselves. Some simply used speed to run away. Others, however, fought back.

Stegosaurus (STEG-OH-SAW-RUS), below, for example, had weapons on its tail — four long, thin, pointed spikes. When **Stegosaurus** was attacked, it would lash its tail around, and the spikes would rip into the flesh of a predator.

Ankylosaurus, as you can see below, had a massive tail-club, one of the strongest weapons of all. Enemies had to beware!

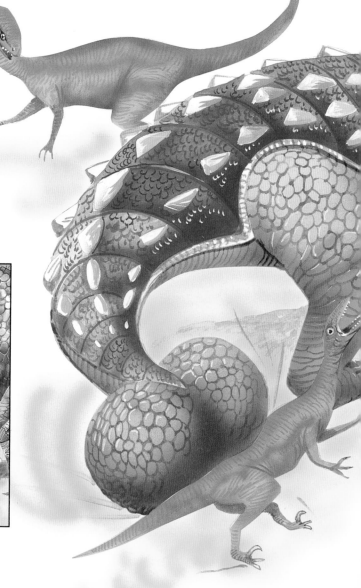

Other dinosaurs, such as **Pachycephalosaurus** (PAK-EE-KEF-AL-OH-SAW-RUS), right, used their heads. The top of its skull looked like a great dome.

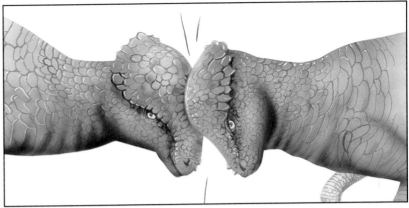

When a predator approached, this dinosaur would charge, threatening to smash into the enemy with its powerful skull.

Triceratops (TRY-SER-A-TOPS), below, used the three horns on its face to fight enemies. Its two main horns measured well over 3 feet (1 m). **Triceratops** would charge at a predator, digging its horns deep into the enemy's flesh. For such a big creature, it was a fast runner. Even the fiercest meat-eaters would have found it difficult to escape.

Scientists also think that **Pachycephalosaurus** had head-banging fights among themselves. They would have fought over mates or to decide who was leader of the group, just like many animals do today.

11

Ankylosaurus discovered

The bones of **Ankylosaurus** were first found in Canada in 1908. The animal was named by a famous dinosaur hunter, Barnum Brown.

Later, Brown heard that there were many dinosaur bones in the cliffs along the Red Deer River in Alberta in western Canada. This made him very curious. He decided to build a big barge for river travel. It was large enough to carry all the members of his expedition.

In the middle of the barge, he pitched a tent to house his scientific laboratory. It even contained a stove. Brown used the barge on many expeditions and often faced some troublesome enemies — swarms of mosquitoes!

Brown and his fellow diggers traveled down the Red Deer River. They stopped whenever they wanted to dig for fossils (the remains of ancient animals). They collected masses of bones from various kinds of dinosaurs that they piled onto the barge.

Among them were the bones of **Ankylosaurus** and **Tyrannosaurus rex**.

Following Brown's success, other scientists traveled the river, looking for dinosaur bones. But, unlike some bone hunters, Brown did not mind others working in the same place. He knew there were more than enough dinosaur bones to go around.

13

The last dinosaurs

It was the start of a new morning in the Cretaceous Period. The weather was mild. As usual, the dinosaurs began their day with a meal. An **Ankylosaurus** chewed on some small, soft ferns.

The biggest meat-eater of the Cretaceous Period was also on the prowl for food. **Tyrannosaurus rex**, huge and frightening, crept through the trees as it hunted prey.

Nearby, an ostrichlike Ornithomimus (OR-NITH-OH-MIME-US) walked past.

Suddenly, it saw a smaller, duck-billed dinosaur, **Parasaurolophus** (PAR-A-SAUR-OH-LOAF-US). This small dinosaur had no chance of escaping the huge jaws of **Tyrannosaurus rex**.

At the water's edge, **Edmontosaurus** (ED-MONT-OH-SAW-RUS) wandered through the ferns. It bit off leaves with its sharp beak and then chewed them with the hundreds of teeth in its cheeks. Up above, reptiles known as pterosaurs flew in the sky. The largest was **Quetzalcoatlus** (KET-SAHL-COAT-LUS), with wings as wide as those of a small airplane.

At first, nothing bothered the animals. Then, they heard a low whistling noise that slowly grew louder and louder.

Lightning flashed. Then came thunder. The dinosaurs stopped eating and looked up.

Suddenly, a great asteroid came whizzing down through the sky, smashing into Earth.

The force of the asteroid as it hit Earth was tremendous. It flung massive amounts of dust high into the sky, blotting out the Sun for years. The world became a dark and cold place. The dinosaurs and pterosaurs were unable to survive the freezing weather, and they soon died out. But this is just one theory about what happened at the end of the age of the dinosaurs. No one knows for sure.

Desert storm

It was a hot, calm day in the Mongolian desert, about 70 million years ago. Two **Saichania** (SY-KA-NIA) were nibbling low plants sticking out of a sand dune. These dinosaurs were smaller cousins of **Ankylosaurus**. They lived far away on what is today the continent of Asia. You can see the family resemblance.

As the dinosaurs ate, the wind began to grow stronger. It lifted the sand from the dune, blowing it high into the air. Within a few minutes, a violent sandstorm was raging.

The **Saichania** were not highly intelligent creatures, but even they realized something was wrong. They stopped nibbling and looked for shelter. But the sand made it difficult for them to see, and there seemed to be nowhere to hide.

Sand swirled around the frightened **Saichania**, getting into their eyes and mouths. In the wind, the sand dune began to move forward like a wave. The dinosaurs did not know what to do, so they stood where they were.

The sand dune moved around them, getting deeper and deeper. Soon, the **Saichania** were trapped. They cried out but could not move. Slowly, the dune covered them. They were buried alive.

After millions of years, paleontologists digging for dinosaur bones in the Mongolian desert came across the fossilized remains of the two unfortunate **Saichania**. Their bones had been preserved in the sand.

17

Self-defense

A fearsome **Tyrannosaurus rex** was on the lookout for food when it spotted an **Ankylosaurus** chewing leaves. Normally, the giant meat-eater would have preferred to attack a smaller dinosaur, but it was feeling especially hungry today. **Tyrannosaurus rex** was not scared of any creature on Earth, and so it decided to attack **Ankylosaurus**.

But the plant-eater was well protected by its body armor, and it had a special weapon.

The only way **Tyrannosaurus rex** could attack **Ankylosaurus** was by charging it and pushing it over onto its back. The plant-eater would not be able to get up by itself, and **Tyrannosaurus rex** would be able to rip open its unprotected belly.

Ankylosaurus heard footsteps and looked up. It immediately knew it was in trouble. There was nowhere to hide, and it did not know if it could outrun **Tyrannosaurus rex**.

Ankylosaurus stood its ground. As soon as the giant **Tyrannosaurus rex** came within range, the brave plant-eater surprised it by attacking first.

Ankylosaurus stood with its head away from the enemy. Then it stepped forward and swung its fearsome tail-club against **Tyrannosaurus rex**'s leg. The great predator roared in pain and surprise and fell backward. It was too late to balance itself. **Tyrannosaurus rex** toppled over and crashed to the ground. The fall broke its leg, and **Tyrannosaurus rex** could not get up. It lay there and groaned as the clever **Ankylosaurus** walked away.

Ankylosaurus and cousins

Ankylosaurus (1) belonged to a group of dinosaurs known as the **Ankylosaurids** (AN-KY-LO-SAW-RIDS). The **Ankylosaurids** lived in several areas of the world during the Cretaceous Period.

Saichania (2) was an **Ankylosaurid** from Mongolia. Its name means "beautiful." But if you had suddenly come face-to-face with this creature, you may not have thought so! It, too, was covered with thick, armored skin and had sharp, triangular spikes on its head and back. But it was a peaceful plant-eater and would not have harmed you — unless attacked.

2

Pinacosaurus (PIN-AK-OH-SAW-RUS) **(3)** was smaller — about the length of a rhinoceros. Its remains have been found in Mongolia. It was well protected with bony spines and had a bony club on the end of its tail.

Pinacosaurus had small teeth and ate soft plants.

Minmi (MIN-MEE) **(4)** is the only known example of an **Ankylosaurid** that has been found in Australia. Very little is known about it. But the picture below shows what it may have looked like, judging by the bones and armored plates that have been found. Scientists think strong back muscles would have helped this creature to run very fast.

1

3

4

Ankylosaurus data

Ankylosaurus had strong armor as protection against attackers. Its tail had powerful muscles for swinging its deadly tail-club. A well-aimed thump could have crippled even the most ferocious predator. But there was one spot on **Ankylosaurus**'s body that was poorly protected — its belly. A powerful attacker would have tried to charge **Ankylosaurus**, knock it on its back, and slash at its belly.

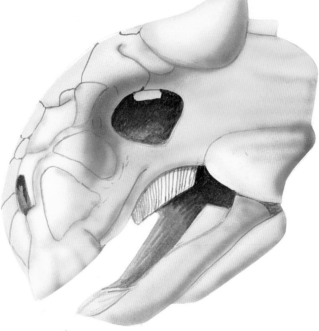

Armor plating

Ankylosaurus's heavy body armor was divided into bands of bone running over its neck, back, and tail. These bands were tough but not stiff. This meant that the animal could move its neck and swing its tail-club easily. Spikes jutting out of the skin gave added protection.

Bony skull

To guard it against its enemies, **Ankylosaurus** had one of the toughest skulls of all the dinosaurs. It was covered with bony sheets that protected its eyes, nostrils, and jaws. The sides of the skull were completely closed in with bone. Small horns stood at the back corners of the skull.

Tail-club

This was a large weapon found on **Ankylosaurus** and its cousins. It was made of two large bones that were fused together. The club had two halves on either side of the tail. This meant it could swipe to the left and the right with this nasty weapon. The club was enormous — about five times wider than a person's head and very heavy. To attack, **Ankylosaurus** kicked its back leg forward and swung its tail at the enemy.

Soft belly

Below **Ankylosaurus**'s heavy body armor lay its soft belly. The belly was not covered by any body armor, so **Ankylosaurus** had to make sure its enemies did not attack it there. However, the lack of armor-plating on the belly and legs gave this dinosaur the ability to take long, fast strides as it ran.

GLOSSARY

armor — a heavy, protective covering.

asteroids — small planets made of rock or metal that orbit, or travel around, the Sun.

carnivores — meat-eating animals.

expedition — a journey or voyage.

predators — animals that kill other animals for food.

prey — animals that are killed for food by other animals.

remains — a dead body or corpse.

reptiles — cold-blooded animals that have hornlike or scaly skin. Lizards, snakes, and turtles are reptiles.

scales — small, thin, platelike parts that cover the skin of fish and reptiles.

INDEX

Ankylosaurids 20, 21

Ankylosaurus: back spines of 7, 9; beak of 8; belly of 7, 22, 23; body armor of 6, 7, 9, 18, 22, 23; bones of 12, 13; claws of 9; eating habits of 5, 9, 14, 18; family of 16, 20; feet of 9; legs of 9; length of 7; neck of 22; and self-defense 10, 18-19; skeleton of 8-9; skin of 6, 9, 22; skull of 9, 23; speed of 9, 23; tail-club of 5, 8, 9, 10, 19, 22, 23; teeth of 8; weight of 7

Brown, Barnum 12, 13

carnivores (meat-eaters) 10, 11, 18

Cretaceous Period 5, 14, 20

disappearance theories 15

Edmontosaurus 15

fossils 13, 17

Minmi 21

Ornithomimus 14

Pachycephalosaurus 11
paleontologists 17
Parasaurolophus 14
Pinacosaurus 21
plant-eaters 5, 18, 19, 21
predators 7, 9, 10, 11, 22
pterosaurs 15

Quetzalcoatlus 15

remains 13

Saichania 16, 17, 20

Triceratops 11
Tyrannosaurus rex 7, 13, 14, 18, 19